D1472790

CHILIES

CHILIES

A Book of Recipes

INTRODUCTION BY JENNY FLEETWOOD

LORENZ BOOKS
NEW YORK • LONDON • SYDNEY • BATH

Lorenz Books is an imprint of
Anness Publishing Limited
27 West 20th Street
New York, New York 10011

LORENZ BOOKS are available for bulk purchase for sales promotion and
for premium use. For details write or call the manager of special sales:
Lorenz Books, 27 West 20th Street, New York, New York 10011: (212) 807-6739.

© 1997 Anness Publishing Limited

ISBN 1 85967 363 5

All rights reserved. No part of this publication may be reproduced, stored in a retrieval system,
or transmitted in any way or by any means, electronic, mechanical, photocopying, recording
or otherwise, without the prior written permission of the copyright holder.

Publisher: Joanna Lorenz
Senior Food Editor: Linda Fraser
Project Editor: Anne Hildyard
Designer: Bill Mason
Illustrations: Anna Koska

Photographers: Karl Adamson, Edward Allwright, David Armstrong, Steve Baxter, James Duncan,
Michelle Garrett, Amanda Heywood, Patrick McLeavey and Thomas Odulate
Recipes: Carla Capalbo, Frances Cleary, Elizabeth Wolf-Cohen, Nicola Diggins, Rafi Fernandez, Sarah Gates,
Shirley Gill, Deh-Ta Hsiung, Shehzad Husain, Sallie Morris, Liz Trigg and Steven Wheeler
Food for photography: Frances Cleary, Elizabeth Wolf-Cohen, Carole Handslip, Jane Hartshorn,
Wendy Lee, Jane Stevenson and Steven Wheeler
Stylists: Maria Kelly and Blake Minton
Cover photography: Janine Hosegood

Printed in China

1 3 5 7 9 10 8 6 4 2

Contents

$\mathcal{I}$NTRODUCTION

Powerhouses of flavor and fire, chilies are wonderful ingredients, well worth exploring in all their many and varied forms. Their reputation as one of the hottest flavorings on the culinary scene is undoubtedly well-deserved, but what is equally true (and perhaps less fully appreciated) is that they can also be subtle. Add a whole chili when cooking a casserole or stew, remove it at the end, and you introduce the merest flicker of flame. To turn up the heat slightly, use sliced medium-hot chilies, defusing them somewhat by scraping out the seeds. Later, if your courage (and your palate) will stand it, go for the burn by cooking with the hottest varieties, leaving the seeds in.

Chilies are native to Central and South America and were a well-kept secret for centuries. It is said that the Aztec emperor Montezuma insisted on having thirty different dishes prepared for him every evening, many of them spiced with one or more of the dozens of varieties of chili available. When the Spanish conquistadores arrived in the sixteenth century, they were struck by how delicious the local food was, and gold was not the only treasure they took with them when they sailed for home.

Europeans embraced chilies – and their mild-mannered relations, sweet bell peppers – with great enthusiasm, and within a very short time they were also introduced to Asia. Today, they add their distinctive flavor to cuisines as diverse as Indian, Malaysian and Thai, and dishes such as Indonesian rijstafel, Hungarian goulash and Austrian paprika schnitzel. In France, that innocuous-looking but lively red mayonnaise that accompanies bouillabaisse is spiked with chilies.

Mexico continues to furnish some of the most exciting and innovative recipes for this magical ingredient. With so many varieties at their disposal, Mexican cooks will often use two types of chili in the same recipe, one selected for its pungency, perhaps, another to add a hint of sweetness.

For years, the only chilies in our markets and supermarkets were the slim tapered red and green serranos or cayennes. However, travelers intrigued by the tastes of spicy dishes in other countries have prompted a need for a wider range of chilies. We can now look forward to getting to know this exciting ingredient better, not only in its fresh form, but also dried, and in sauces, salsas and pickles. Take the chili challenge – and add an exciting twist to your cooking.

Jenny Fleetwood

TYPES OF CHILI

ANAHEIM

These large Mexican chilies are mild to medium hot. They can be stuffed or used in sauces, stews and salsas.

JALAPENO

Available green or red, fresh or pickled, jalapeños are hot and are used in tamales, salsas and sauces.

HABANERO

Also known as Scotch Bonnet, these chilies are extremely hot. They are used in Caribbean jerk sauces.

THAI

These tiny chilies are fairly hot and are used in Thai curry paste and salads.

ANCHO

These are dried and are mild and quite sweet.

CASCABEL

Round, dried cascabel chilies rattle when shaken.

CHIPOTLE

The dried, smoked versions of jalapeño chilies, chipotle chilies give an intense heat to soups or stews.

GUAJILLO

Fairly mild in flavor, and very good with seafood.

TEPIN

Tiny and blisteringly hot, tepin chilies are used to make hot pepper sauce for Thai cuisine.

INDIAN

Small and very hot, these are used in curries.

CAYENNE, HOT CHILI POWDER AND CHILI FLAKES

Cayenne is a pungent spice made from blended red chilies, chili powder can be ground chilies or a special mix, and chili flakes are crushed dried chilies. All are used to spice up sausages, sauces and oils.

MINCED CHILI, CHILI OIL AND HOT RED PEPPER SAUCE

Minced chili is a paste made from ground red chilies. Chili oil is good for frying, or basting meat or fish on the barbecue. Hot red pepper sauce is very popular in Malaysian and Caribbean cuisine.

Jalapeño

Cayenne

Hot chili powder

Chili flakes

Ancho

Indian

Habanero

Anaheim

Tepin

Thai

Cascabel

Guajillo

Minced chili

Chili oil

Hot red pepper sauce

Chipotle

$\mathcal{B}$ASIC $\mathcal{T}$ECHNIQUES

PREPARING CHILIES

The oil in chilies contains a chemical, capsaicin, which is a strong irritant, so it is vital to handle chilies with care. Work in a well-ventilated area and wear gloves, if possible. To prepare, slit chilies lengthwise with a sharp knife. Scrape out the seeds.

Slice the chilies or chop them finely. Much of the heat is concentrated in the seeds, so you may prefer to discard some or all of them. If you have worked without gloves, wash your hands several times in soapy water. Avoid touching your face, especially the eye area.

"FIRE" EXTINGUISHERS
If you have managed to get chili oil on delicate skin, an alkali such as a paste made from bicarbonate of soda and water will help to ease the discomfort. If you inadvertently chomp on a chili and feel as though your mouth is on fire, reach for bread, rice, plain yogurt or milk. Whatever you do, avoid sparkling water or any other fizzy drink, or your tongue will feel as if someone is using it for target practice.

CHOOSING CHILIES

• Fresh chilies should be firm, glossy and evenly colored. Avoid musty or soft chilies.

• If fresh chilies are not available, use canned ones, but taste a tiny portion to judge the heat and therefore the quantity required.

• It is a good idea to buy dried chilies in transparent packaging, so that you can see the quality at a glance.

• If dried chilies look a little dusty when you remove them from the packaging, don't worry. Just wipe them gently with a paper towel before use.

• Chili flakes and ground chilies should have good aroma and color. If chili powder looks dark, this is not a sign that it is stale, rather an indication that the chilies have been mixed with other spices, American-style.

STORING CHILIES

• The best way to store fresh chilies is to wrap them well in paper towels, place them in a plastic bag, and keep them in a drawer of your fridge. They will keep well for a week or more, but it is a good idea to check

them occasionally and discard any that begin to show signs of softening.

• Chilies can also be frozen. There is no need to blanch them if you plan to use them fairly quickly.

• Store ground chilies in airtight jars in a cool place out of direct sunlight. Buy small quantities and use as soon as possible. Some cooks store dried chilies (and curry powder) in the freezer.

• To dry your own fresh chilies, thread them on a string, hang them in a warm, dry place until they are crumbly, then crush them in a mortar and pestle.

• Pack chilies in a sterilized jar and pour sherry over them to cover. Close tightly and store in a cool, dark place. You can use both the chilies and the sherry for flavoring.

MAKING A CHILI FLOWER

Chili flowers make a very pretty garnish. Carefully slit each chili lengthwise and scrape out the seeds, taking care not to damage the flesh. Keeping the chili intact at the stem end, cut it into as many fine strips as possible.

Drop the chilies into a bowl of ice water, cover and chill for several hours. The ice water will make the chili strips curl back. Drain well on paper towels and garnish the food with the chilies just before serving. Chili flowers are not edible.

CHILI RELISH

Make this at least 1 hour before serving to allow the flavors to blend. Finely chop 2 large tomatoes. Place them in a mixing bowl.

Chop 1 red onion and 1 garlic clove. Add to the tomatoes, mix well, then stir in 2 teaspoons chili sauce (use a sweet chili sauce or a hot one, as desired).

Stir in 1 tablespoon chopped fresh basil and 1 chopped green chili – with the seeds if you want a hot relish – then add a pinch each of salt and sugar.

COOK'S TIPS

• Unless chilies are very thin-skinned, they will benefit from being peeled. Char them under a hot broiler, or by turning them in a gas flame. Put the hot chilies in a bowl, cover with several layers of paper towels and let sit for 10 minutes. Rub off the skin with gloved fingers or scrape with a sharp knife.

• To reduce the heat of fresh or dried chilies, soak them for an hour in a solution of wine vinegar and salt in the ratio 3:1.

• To bring out the flavor of chilies, dry roast them in a hot non-stick frying pan for a few minutes. Do not let them change color.

• Chili and cheese make perfect partners. Stir about 1 teaspoon sweet chili sauce (or a seeded roasted chili) into 1 cup grated aged Cheddar cheese, then beat in an egg. Toast bread on one side only, pile the cheese mixture on the untoasted side and broil until puffy and golden.

HARISSA

For a delicious taste, brush a small amount of this fiery North African sauce over chicken wings before grilling them. In its country of origin, harissa is used as a condiment with meat or rice dishes.

Remove the seeds from 4 ounces dried red chilies, then soak them in warm water to cover until soft. Drain well. Using scissors, snip the chilies into chunks, then pound them to a paste with a mortar and pestle. Add 4 chopped garlic cloves, ½ teaspoon salt, 1 tablespoon ground cumin and 2 teaspoons each of dried mint and caraway seeds. Grind to a paste, then stir in 4 tablespoons olive oil. Scrape into a sterilized jar, cover with a layer of olive oil and chill. It can be kept in the fridge for up to 6 weeks.

PICKLED CHILIES

Here are two excellent ways of dealing with an excess of fresh chilies. The easiest way to pickle chilies is to slit them, remove the seeds and pack them in sterilized jars with spiced vinegar to cover. Alternatively, cut off the tops, leaving the cores and seeds intact, then slice the chilies in half horizontally. Blanch them in a 50:50 mixture of white vinegar and water with a little salt. Let it cool, then pack into sterilized jars, tucking whole peeled garlic cloves between the layers. Fill the jars with olive oil, close tightly and let steep for at least 2 weeks before using.

ROUILLE   *Traditionally added to bouillabaisse, this is a French red chili mayonnaise.*

Peel and seed 1 fresh red chili, then pound it to a paste with 2 garlic cloves. Scrape the mixture into a bowl and add 2 egg yolks, a pinch of salt and pepper, 1 teaspoon red pepper mustard and 1 tablespoon lemon juice. Whisk in ¼ teaspoon cayenne pepper. Have ready 1 cup of equal quantities of olive oil and sunflower oil. Whisking constantly, add the oil to the mixture, drop by drop, then in a slow stream. Makes 1¼ cups.

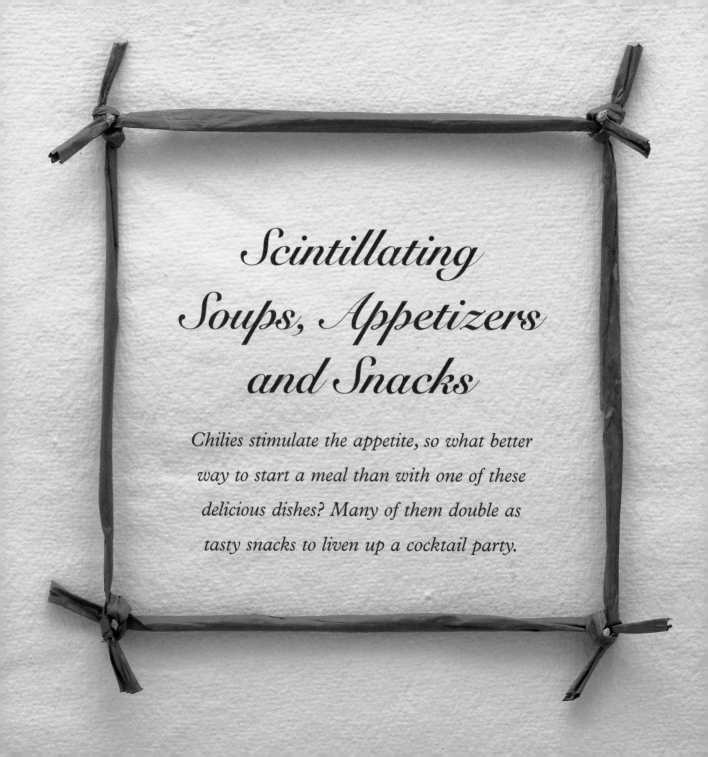

Scintillating Soups, Appetizers and Snacks

Chilies stimulate the appetite, so what better way to start a meal than with one of these delicious dishes? Many of them double as tasty snacks to liven up a cocktail party.

SHRIMP, MINT AND CHILI SALAD

Coconut milk and lime juice tame the fiery taste of chilies in this superb salad.

Serves 4

12 large shrimp, thawed if frozen

1 tablespoon butter

1 tablespoon fish sauce

juice of 1 lime

3 tablespoons thin coconut milk

1 teaspoon superfine sugar

1 garlic clove, crushed

1-inch piece fresh ginger,
*   peeled and grated*

2 fresh red chilies, seeded and
*   finely chopped*

2 tablespoons fresh mint leaves

ground black pepper

coconut strips, to garnish

8 ounces lettuce leaves, to serve

COOK'S TIP
This makes a warm salad, but the shrimp will have a better flavor if left to marinate in the sauce for 1 hour.

Peel the shrimp, leaving the tails intact. Slit the back of each shrimp, working from the tail to the head, and remove the black vein.

Melt the butter in a large frying pan and add the shrimp. Toss them over the heat until they turn pink.

Mix the fish sauce, lime juice, coconut milk, sugar, garlic, ginger and chilies in a bowl. Add black pepper to taste. Add the warm shrimp to the sauce with the mint leaves. Toss and let marinate. Serve the shrimp mixture on a bed of lettuce leaves garnished with coconut strips.

TORTILLA AND CHILI SOUP

This tasty soup, with fresh green chilies and tortillas, has more than a hint of Mexican flavor.

Serves 4

1 onion, finely chopped

1 garlic clove, crushed

1 tablespoon vegetable oil

2 tomatoes, peeled, seeded
  and chopped

½ teaspoon salt

10 cups chicken stock

1 carrot, diced

1 small zucchini, diced

1 boneless chicken breast, cooked,
  skinned and finely sliced

2 green chilies, seeded and chopped

For the garnish

4 corn tortillas

oil for frying

1 ripe avocado, peeled, pitted
  and diced

2 scallions, chopped

2 tablespoons chopped fresh cilantro

Fry the onion and garlic in the oil for 5-8 minutes. Add the tomatoes and salt and cook for 5 minutes. Add the stock, bring to a boil, then simmer, covered, for about 15 minutes. Meanwhile, for the garnish, cut the tortillas into strips. Pour about ½ inch of oil into a frying pan and heat until the oil is hot. Add the tortilla strips in batches and fry until they just begin to brown. Remove with a slotted spoon and drain on paper towels. Add the carrot to the soup and cook, covered, for 10 minutes. Add the zucchini, chicken and chilies and cook, uncovered, for 5 minutes. Divide the tortilla strips and avocado among four soup bowls. Ladle in the soup, then scatter the scallions and cilantro on top. Serve immediately.

BEEF CHILI SOUP

Based on a traditional recipe, this hearty soup with fresh red chilies makes a warming start to any meal.
Serve it with plenty of crusty bread.

Serves 4

1 tablespoon vegetable oil

1 onion, chopped

6 ounces ground beef

2 garlic cloves, chopped

1 fresh red chili, sliced

¼ cup flour

14-ounce can chopped tomatoes

2½ cups beef stock

1¾ cups drained, canned kidney
   beans

salt and ground black pepper

2 tablespoons chopped fresh parsley,
   to garnish

crusty bread, to serve

COOK'S TIP

For a milder flavor, remove the
seeds from the chili after you
have sliced it.

Heat the oil in a large saucepan. Add the onion and ground beef and fry for 5 minutes, until brown and sealed. Stir the mixture frequently.

Stir in the garlic, chili and flour. Cook for 1 minute. Add the tomatoes and pour in the stock. Bring to a boil, stirring constantly.

Stir in the kidney beans and season with plenty of salt and pepper. Cook for 20 more minutes.

Check the seasoning, then pour into heated soup bowls. Sprinkle with fresh parsley and serve immediately with crusty bread.

STEAMED CHILI MUSSELS

This is a glorious treat for all lovers of spicy seafood. If you like your food extra hot, simply add more fresh chilies to taste.

Serves 6

2 fresh chilies

6 ripe tomatoes

2 tablespoons peanut oil

2 garlic cloves, crushed

2 shallots, finely chopped

2¼ pounds fresh mussels, scrubbed
   and beards removed

2 tablespoons white wine

2 tablespoons chopped fresh parsley,
   to garnish

French bread, to serve (optional)

COOK'S TIP

When preparing the mussels, discard any that are not tightly closed, or which do not snap shut if you tap them sharply. The opposite rule applies to the cooked mussels. Discard any that fail to open.

Chop the fresh chilies roughly and remove the seeds. Chop the tomatoes into small pieces.

Heat the peanut oil in a large, heavy saucepan and gently sauté the garlic and shallots until soft. Stir in the tomatoes and chili and simmer for 10 minutes.

Add the prepared mussels and white wine to the saucepan, cover tightly and cook, shaking the pan frequently, for about 5 minutes, or until all the mussel shells have opened. Scatter the chopped parsley on top. Serve in a large bowl with chunks of fresh French bread, if desired.

GARLIC CHILI SHRIMP

Served piping hot and sizzling with flavor, these Spanish-style shrimp are stir-fried in olive oil spiced with fresh red chili and garlic to make a delicious appetizer.

Serves 4

¼ cup olive oil

2–3 garlic cloves, finely chopped

1 fresh red chili, seeded and chopped

16 cooked large shrimp

1 tablespoon chopped fresh parsley

salt and ground black pepper

lemon wedges and flat-leaf parsley,
   to garnish

French bread, to serve (optional)

COOK'S TIP

Add a dash or two of Tabasco just before serving the shrimp, if desired.

Heat the oil in a large frying pan and add the garlic and chili. Stir-fry for 1 minute, until the garlic begins to turn brown.

Add the shrimp and stir-fry for 3–4 minutes, coating them well with the flavored oil. Add salt and pepper to taste.

Sprinkle in the parsley, remove from the heat and place the shrimp in a heated serving bowl. Pour the flavored oil over them. Serve with French bread to mop up the juices, if desired. Garnish the shrimp with lemon wedges and flat leaf parsley.

DEEP-FRIED WONTONS WITH CHILI SAMBAL

The sambal, a spicy sauce made with fresh red chilies, makes a hot and fiery dip for these delicious crisp appetizers. You can prepare the wontons in advance and freeze them.

Makes 40

4 ounces pork loin, trimmed
    and sliced
8 ounces cooked shrimp, peeled
    and deveined
2–3 garlic cloves, crushed
2 scallions, roughly chopped
1 tablespoon cornstarch
about 40 wonton wrappers
oil, for deep-frying
salt and ground black pepper

For the chili sambal

1–2 fresh red chilies, seeded
    and sliced
1–2 garlic cloves, crushed
3 tablespoons dark soy sauce
3–4 tablespoons lemon or lime juice

Grind the slices of pork finely in a food processor or blender. Add the shrimp, garlic, scallions and cornstarch. Season to taste and then process briefly.

Position the wonton wrapper in front of you like a diamond. Place a little of the prepared filling on each wrapper, just off center. Dampen all the edges with water, except for the uppermost corner of the diamond.

Lift the corner nearest you toward the filling and then roll up the wrapper once, to cover the filling. Turn over. Bring the two far corners together, sealing one on top of the other. Squeeze lightly, to plump up the filling. Repeat until all the wrappers and filling have been used up. Set the filled wontons aside.

Prepare the sambal. Mix the chilies and garlic in a bowl, then stir in the dark soy sauce and the lemon juice. Add enough water (1–2 tablespoons) to make a dipping sauce. Pour the sambal into a small serving bowl and set aside.

Heat the oil in a deep-fryer to 375°F or until a cube of day-old bread browns in 30 seconds. Deep-fry the filled wontons in batches for 2–3 minutes or until cooked through, crisp and golden brown. Remove with a slotted spoon and drain on paper towels. If frozen, they will need about 4 minutes. Serve on a large platter, with the chili sambal.

TORTILLA TURNOVERS WITH CHEESE AND CHILI FILLING

These delicious fried turnovers, spiced with jalapeño chilies, come from Mexico, where they are called Quesadillas. *This size makes a popular snack and smaller versions can be served as canapés.*

Makes 14
14 freshly prepared unbaked tortillas

For the filling
*2 cups finely chopped or grated
   Cheddar cheese*
*3 fresh jalapeño chilies, seeded and
   cut into strips*
oil, for shallow frying
salt
shredded lettuce, to serve

COOK'S TIP
*For other stuffing ideas, try
leftover beans with chilies, or
chopped chorizo sausage, fried
with a little chopped onion.*

Combine the cheese and chili in a bowl. Season with salt and set aside. Heat the oil in a frying pan. Hold an unbaked tortilla in the palm of your hand and put a spoonful of filling along the center, avoiding the edges.

Fold the tortilla and seal the edges by pressing or crimping together. Put it in the hot oil. Repeat with two more tortillas, or as many as the frying pan will hold. Fry each batch until golden brown and crisp on both sides.

Using a spatula, lift out the turnovers and drain them on paper towels. Transfer to a plate and keep hot. Serve immediately on a bed of lettuce.

NACHOS WITH CHILI BEEF

Tortilla chips spiced up with a red chili and ground beef topping make an irresistible appetizer or snack.

Serves 4

8 ounces ground beef

2 fresh red chilies, sliced

3 scallions, chopped

6 ounces tortilla chips

1¼ cups sour cream

½ cup grated
    Cheddar cheese

salt and ground black pepper

Dry-fry the ground beef and chilies in a large frying pan for 10 minutes, stirring constantly, then add the scallions and cook for 5 more minutes. Stir in salt and pepper to taste. Preheat the broiler.

Arrange the chips in four individual flameproof dishes. Spoon on the ground beef mixture, then top with the sour cream and grated cheese. Broil under medium heat for 5 minutes. Serve immediately.

COOK'S TIP

Use finely chopped dill pickles instead of scallions, and Monterey Jack instead of Cheddar cheese, if desired.

23

CORN FRITTERS WITH CHILI SALSA

The chili salsa adds piquancy to the lightly spiced fritters.

Makes about 48

corn or other vegetable oil

3 cups canned corn

1 cup flour

½ cup cornmeal

1 cup milk

2 teaspoons baking powder

2 teaspoons sugar

1 teaspoon salt

½ teaspoon grated nutmeg

½ teaspoon cayenne pepper

4 eggs, lightly beaten

lettuce, cherry tomatoes and fresh cilantro, to serve

For the salsa

4 ounces cherry tomatoes, chopped

¾ cup canned corn

1 red bell pepper, finely chopped

½ small red onion, finely chopped

juice of 1 lemon

2 tablespoons olive oil

2 tablespoons chopped fresh cilantro

1–2 fresh chilies, seeded and finely chopped

Prepare the salsa at least 2 hours in advance. Drain the corn, then combine all the ingredients in a medium-size bowl, crushing them lightly with the back of a spoon to release the juices. Cover and refrigerate until ready to use.

Put 2 tablespoons of the oil in a medium-size bowl. Add the corn (drained), flour, cornmeal, milk, baking powder, sugar, salt, nutmeg, cayenne and eggs. Mix until just blended; do not overbeat. If the batter is too stiff, stir in a little more milk or water. Unless you plan to serve the fritters as soon as they are cooked, preheat the oven to 325°F.

Heat oil to a depth of ½ inch in a large heavy frying pan until hot but not smoking. Drop tablespoons of batter into the hot oil, a few at a time, and cook for 3–4 minutes, until golden, turning once. Remove with a slotted spoon and drain on paper towels. Arrange the corn fritters on a serving plate and top each one with a spoonful of salsa. Serve immediately with lettuce, tomatoes and cilantro. Alternatively, arrange the fritters on baking sheets and keep them warm for up to 1 hour in the oven.

MEXICAN DIP WITH CHILI CHIPS

Fresh red chili gives a hint of heat to the avocado dip, and the chips are fired up with chili powder.

Serves 4

2 ripe avocados

juice of 1 lime

½ small onion, finely chopped

½ fresh red chili, seeded and
*   finely chopped*

3 tomatoes, peeled, seeded
*   and chopped*

2 tablespoons chopped fresh cilantro

2 tablespoons sour cream

salt and ground black pepper

1 tablespoon sour cream and
*   a pinch of cayenne pepper,*
*   to garnish*

For the chips

5 ounces tortilla chips

2 tablespoons finely grated aged
*   Cheddar cheese*

¼ teasoon chili powder

2 tablespoons chopped fresh parsley

Cut the avocados in half, remove the pits and scoop out the flesh with a spoon, scraping the shells well.

Place the flesh in a blender or food processor. Add the lime juice, chopped onion, chili, tomatoes, chopped cilantro and sour cream, with salt to taste and a generous grinding of black pepper. Process until fairly smooth. Scrape into a bowl, cover tightly and place in the fridge until needed.

Meanwhile, preheat the broiler, then scatter the tortilla chips over a baking sheet. Mix the grated Cheddar cheese with the chili powder, sprinkle the mixture over the chips, and broil for 1–2 minutes, until the cheese has melted. Sprinkle with the parsley.

Remove the avocado dip from the fridge, top with the sour cream and sprinkle with cayenne pepper. Serve the bowl on a large plate surrounded by the chili tortilla chips.

Fiery Main Meals

Many of the world's finest chili dishes come from India and Thailand: some are fast and fiery; others spicy and subtle. Here are some favorites, with contributions from other countries too.

SALMON WITH SPICY CHILI PESTO

The pesto is unusual because it uses sunflower seeds and fresh red chilies as its flavorings rather than the classic basil and pine nuts.

Serves 4

4 salmon steaks, 8 ounces each
2 tablespoons sunflower oil
finely grated rind and juice of 1 lime
lime wedges, to serve

For the spicy chili pesto
6 mild fresh red chilies, seeded
2 garlic cloves
2 tablespoons sunflower seeds
  or pumpkin seeds
finely grated rind and juice of 1 lime
5 tablespoons olive oil
salt and ground black pepper

COOK'S TIP

For a fast supper, you can pay a little more and buy salmon fillet. If you do have time, try this method of boning steaks.

Insert a sharp knife close to the top of the bone of a salmon steak. Working close to the bone, cut your way to the end of the steak until one side of the steak has been released and one side is still attached. Repeat with the other side. Pull out any visible bones with a pair of tweezers. Cut away the skin in one piece. Form each piece of fish into a circle, with the thinner end wrapped around the fatter end. Secure tightly with a length of string.

Rub oil into the fish. Add the lime rind and juice and chill for 2 hours.

To make the pesto, process the chilies, garlic, seeds, lime rind, lime juice and seasoning in a food processor or blender until well mixed. With the motor running, gradually add the oil through the feeder tube until the sauce has thickened and emulsified. Preheat the oven to 350°F. Drain the salmon and cook for 5 minutes on each side. Serve with the pesto and lime wedges.

STEAMED FISH WITH CHILI SAUCE

This sweet chili sauce is delicious, but can come as a bit of a shock to the uninitiated. If you are unaccustomed to fiery flavors, reduce the number of red chilies.

Serves 4

1 large fish, or 2 medium firm fish,
   such as bass or grouper, scaled
   and cleaned
1 fresh banana leaf
2 tablespoons rice wine
3 fresh red chilies, seeded and
   finely sliced
2 garlic cloves, finely chopped
¾-inch piece fresh ginger,
   finely shredded
2 lemongrass stalks, crushed and
   finely chopped
2 scallions, chopped
2 tablespoons fish sauce
juice of 1 lime

For the chili sauce

10 red chilies, seeded and chopped
4 garlic cloves, chopped
¼ cup fish sauce
1 tablespoon sugar
5 tablespoons lime juice

Rinse the fish inside and out under cold running water. Pat dry with paper towels. With a sharp knife, slash the skin of the fish a few times on both sides.

Place the fish on the banana leaf. Mix all the remaining ingredients and spread over the fish.

Place a small upturned plate in the bottom of a wok and pour in boiling water to a depth of 2 inches. Lift the banana leaf, with the fish, and support it on the plate in the wok. Cover with a lid. Steam for 10–15 minutes or until the fish is cooked.

Meanwhile, place all the ingredients for the chili sauce in a food processor or blender and process until smooth. You may need to add a little cold water.

Serve the fish hot, on the banana leaf if desired, with the sweet chili sauce in a bowl to spoon over the top.

MONKFISH WITH GREEN CHILI SALSA

Marinated monkfish is doubly delicious served Mexican-style, with a spicy green chili salsa.

Serves 4

1½ pounds monkfish tail

3 tablespoons olive oil

2 tablespoons lime juice

1 garlic clove, crushed

1 tablespoon chopped fresh cilantro

salt and ground black pepper

cilantro sprigs and lime slices,

  to garnish

For the green chili salsa

4 tomatoes

1 avocado

½ red onion, chopped

1 green chili, seeded and chopped

2 tablespoons chopped fresh cilantro

2 tablespoons olive oil

1 tablespoon lime juice

To make the salsa, cut a cross in the top of each of the tomatoes. Dip them in boiling water for 30 seconds, then drain, peel off the skins and dice the flesh. Cut the avocado in half, and remove the pit and peel. Dice the avocado flesh. Mix the tomatoes, avocado, onion, chili, cilantro, olive oil and lime juice in a bowl. Cover and let sit at room temperature for about 40 minutes.

Meanwhile, prepare the monkfish. Using a sharp knife, remove the pinkish-gray membrane. Cut the fillets from either side of the backbone, then cut each fillet in half to make four steaks.

Mix the oil, lime juice, garlic and cilantro in a shallow non-metallic dish. Add a little salt and pepper, then lay the monkfish steaks in the dish. Turn them several times to coat with the marinade, then cover the dish and marinate the fish at a cool room temperature or in the fridge for 30 minutes. Preheat the broiler.

Drain the monkfish, reserving the marinade. Broil for 10–12 minutes, turning once and brushing regularly with the marinade, until the steaks are cooked through.

Serve the monkfish garnished with cilantro sprigs and lime slices and accompanied by the green chili salsa.

CHICKEN WITH CHILIES AND CASHEWS

Chicken with red chilies, cashews and a touch of garlic makes for a delicious stir-fry.

Serves 4–6

1 pound chicken breasts, boned and
  skinned
2 tablespoons vegetable oil
2 garlic cloves, sliced
4 dried red chilies, chopped
1 red bell pepper, seeded and cut into
  ¾-inch dice
2 tablespoons oyster sauce
1 tablespoon soy sauce
pinch of sugar
1 bunch scallions, cut into
  2-inch lengths
1½ cups cashews, roasted
fresh cilantro leaves, to garnish

With a sharp knife, cut the chicken into bite-size pieces. Heat a wok, add the oil and swirl it around gently. Add the garlic and dried chilies and fry until the garlic is golden.

Add the chicken and stir-fry until it changes color, then add the red bell pepper. If necessary, moisten with a little water.

Stir in the oyster sauce, soy sauce and sugar. Add the scallions and cashews. Stir–fry for 1–2 more minutes. Serve, garnished with fresh cilantro leaves.

CHICKEN IN ALMOND AND CHILI SAUCE

Green bell pepper and jalapeño chili combine with tomatillos to make this popular Mexican dish.

Serves 6

*3-3½ pounds chicken, cut into
    serving pieces*

2 cups chicken stock

1 onion, chopped

1 garlic clove, chopped

2 cups fresh cilantro, roughly chopped

*1 green bell pepper, seeded and
    chopped*

1 jalapeño chili, seeded and chopped

*10-ounce can tomatillos (Mexican
    green tomatoes)*

1 cup ground almonds

2 tablespoons corn oil

salt

fresh cilanto sprig, to garnish

rice, to serve

Put the chicken pieces into a shallow pan with the stock. Bring to a simmer, cover and cook for about 45 minutes, until tender. Drain the stock into a measuring pitcher and set aside.

Put the onion, garlic, cilantro, pepper, chili, tomatillos with their juice and the almonds in a food processor or blender. Purée fairly coarsely.

Heat the oil in a frying pan, add the almond mixture and cook over low heat, stirring for 3–4 minutes. Scrape into the pan with the chicken.

Make the stock up to 2 cups with water, if necessary. Stir it into the pan. Mix gently and simmer for just long enough to blend the flavors and heat the chicken pieces through. Add salt to taste. Serve immediately, garnished with cilantro and accompanied by rice.

COCONUT CHICKEN WITH GREEN CHILI PASTE

This green curry, from Thailand, owes its delicious spicy flavor to fresh green chilies.

Serves 4–6

2½ -pound chicken, without giblets

2½ cups coconut milk

1¾ cups chicken stock

2 lime leaves

2 teaspoons coriander seeds

½ teaspoon cumin seeds

4 fresh green chilies, finely chopped

4 teaspoons sugar

2 teaspoons salt

3-inch piece lemongrass

2 tablespoons chopped fresh ginger

3 garlic cloves, crushed

1 onion, finely chopped

¾-inch piece dried shrimp paste

3 tablespoons each chopped cilantro
   leaves and chopped fresh mint

½ teaspoon ground nutmeg

2 tablespoons vegetable oil

1 sweet potato, peeled and diced

1 small butternut squash, peeled,
   seeded and roughly chopped

4 ounces green beans

fresh cilantro, to garnish

Cut the chicken into serving pieces. Remove the skin. Strain the coconut milk into a bowl, reserving the solids in the strainer. Place the chicken in a pan, cover with the thin coconut milk and the stock. Add the lime leaves and simmer, uncovered, for 40 minutes. Lift out the chicken, take it off the bone and set it aside.

To make the paste, dry-fry the seeds in a wok. Using a mortar and pestle, grind the chilies with the sugar and salt to make a smooth paste. Add the seeds from the wok, lemongrass, ginger, garlic and onion, then grind smoothly. Add the shrimp paste, herbs, nutmeg and oil and mix well.

Place a ladleful of the chicken cooking liquid in a large wok. Add 4–5 tablespoons of the curry paste to the liquid, according to taste. Mix well. Boil rapidly until the liquid has reduced completely. Add the remaining cooking liquid with the chicken, sweet potato, squash and beans (trimmed and halved). Simmer for 10–15 minutes until the sweet potato is cooked. Just before serving, stir in the thick part of the coconut milk and simmer gently to thicken. Serve garnished with shredded cilantro.

CHILI PORK RIBS WITH GREEN BEANS

A pungent chili paste made from dried red chilies gives this stir-fry an unforgettable flavor.

Serves 4–6

1½ pound pork spare ribs
  (or pork belly)
2 tablespoons vegetable oil
1 tablespoon sugar
1 tablespoon fish sauce
1 cup fine green beans, trimmed and
  cut into 2-inch lengths
2 kaffir lime leaves, finely sliced
2 fresh red chilies, finely sliced,
  to garnish

For the chili paste

3 dried red chilies, seeded
  and soaked
4 shallots, chopped
4 garlic cloves, chopped
1 teaspoon chopped galangal
  or fresh ginger
1 lemongrass stalk, chopped
6 black peppercorns
1 teaspoon shrimp paste
2 tablespoons dried shrimp, rinsed

Put all the ingredients for the chili paste in a mortar and grind with a pestle until the mixture forms a thick paste.

Slice and chop the spare ribs or pork belly into 1½-inch lengths.

Heat the oil in a wok or large frying pan. Add the pork and fry for about 5 minutes, until lightly browned.

Stir in the chili paste and continue to cook for 5 more minutes, stirring constantly to prevent the paste from sticking to the pan.

Pour in ½ cup water, cover and simmer for 7–10 minutes or until the spare ribs are tender. Stir in the sugar and fish sauce and taste to check the seasoning.

Add the green beans and kaffir lime leaves and fry until the beans are cooked. Serve garnished with sliced red chilies.

Stir-fried Beef in Oyster and Chili Sauce

Red chilies add tongue-tingling heat to this tasty beef stir-fry.

Serves 4–6

1 pound rump steak

2 tablespoons soy sauce

1 tablespoon cornstarch

3 tablespoons vegetable oil

1 tablespoon chopped garlic

1 tablespoon chopped fresh ginger

2 cups mixed mushrooms such as
    shiitake, oyster and straw

1 tablespoon oyster sauce

1 tablespoon sweet chili sauce

1 teaspoon sugar

ground black pepper

4 scallions, cut into short lengths

2 red chilies, seeded and cut
    into strips

COOK'S TIP

*Made from extracts of oysters,
oyster sauce is smooth with a
savory-sweet and meaty taste.*

Slice the beef on the diagonal into long thin strips. Mix the soy sauce and cornstarch in a large bowl, stir in the beef, cover and let marinate for 1–2 hours.

Heat half the oil in a wok or large frying pan. Add the garlic and ginger and fry until fragrant. Stir in the beef. Stir to separate the strips, let them color, then cook for 1–2 minutes. Remove from the wok and set aside.

Heat the remaining oil in the wok. Add the shiitake, oyster and straw mushrooms. Stir-fry until tender.

Return the beef to the wok and mix it with the mushrooms. Add the oyster sauce, chili sauce and sugar, with black pepper to taste. Mix well, then add the scallions and red chilies. Stir to mix. Serve immediately.

MADRAS CURRY

Fresh green and red chilies add bite to this medium-hot curry.

Serves 4–6

¼ cup vegetable oil

1 large onion, finely sliced

3–4 cloves

4 green cardamom pods, bruised

2 whole star anise

4 fresh green chilies, chopped

2 fresh red chilies, chopped

3 tablespoons Madras curry paste

1 teaspoon ground turmeric

1 pound lean beef, cubed

¼ cup tamarind juice

salt and sugar, to taste

fresh cilantro sprig, to garnish

COOK'S TIP

If the curry is a little too hot for your taste, just spoon a dollop of plain yogurt or raita (yogurt and cucumber sambal) on the top.

Heat the oil in a flameproof casserole and fry the onion until golden brown. Lower the heat, and add the cloves, cardamom, star anise, chilies, curry paste and turmeric. Mix well. Fry for another 2–3 minutes.

Add the beef and mix well to coat it in the spices. Cover and cook over low heat for 1 hour, or until the beef is tender, stirring occasionally. Increase the heat and cook, uncovered, for a few more minutes to reduce any excess cooking liquid.

Stir in the tamarind juice, with salt and sugar to taste. Reheat the dish and serve hot, garnished with the fresh cilantro.

PORK CHOPS WITH SOUR GREEN CHILI SALSA

Roasted chilies are the secret of this salsa's success. It is particularly good with pork but could also be served with chicken or shrimp.

Serves 4

2 tablespoons vegetable oil

1 tablespoon fresh lemon juice

2 teaspoons ground cumin

1 teaspoon dried oregano

8 pork loin chops, about
*   ¾-inch thick*

salt and ground black pepper

lettuce, chopped tomatoes and pepper,
*   to serve*

For the salsa

2 fresh hot green chilies

2 green bell peppers, chopped

1 tomato, peeled and seeded

½ onion, roughly chopped

4 scallions

1 drained pickled jalapeño chili,
*   stem removed*

2 teaspoons olive oil

2 teaspoons fresh lime juice

3 teaspoons cider vinegar

1 teaspoon salt

Combine the vegetable oil, lemon juice, cumin and oregano in a small bowl. Add pepper to taste and stir to mix.

Arrange the pork chops in one layer in a shallow dish, brushing each chop with the oil mixture on both sides. Cover and let stand for 2–3 hours at a cool room temperature, or overnight in the fridge.

To make the salsa, roast the chilies over a gas flame, holding them with tongs, until charred on all sides. (Alternatively, char the skins under the broiler.) Let cool for 5 minutes. Wearing rubber gloves, remove the charred skin. For a less fiery flavor, discard the seeds.

Place the chilies in a food processor or blender. Add the remaining salsa ingredients. Process until finely chopped; do not purée.

Transfer the salsa to a heavy saucepan and simmer for about 15 minutes, stirring occasionally. Set aside.

Season the pork chops. Heat a ridged pan. (Alternatively, preheat the broiler.) When hot, add the pork chops and cook for about 5 minutes, until browned. Turn and continue cooking for 5–7 more minutes or until cooked through. Work in batches, if necessary. Serve immediately, with the sour green chili salsa, lettuce, chopped tomatoes and pepper.

CHILI, TOMATO AND SPINACH PIZZA

This richly flavored topping with fresh chilies makes a tasty and satisfying pizza.

Serves 3

*3 tablespoons tomato oil (from jar of
    sun-dried tomatoes)*

1 onion, chopped

2 garlic cloves, chopped

*1-2 fresh chilies, seeded and
    finely chopped*

*4 drained sun-dried tomatoes in oil,
    roughly chopped*

14-ounce can chopped tomatoes

1 tablespoon tomato paste

6 ounces fresh spinach

1 pizza crust, 10-12 inch

*3 ounces smoked mozzarella
    cheese, grated*

¾ cup grated aged Cheddar cheese

salt and ground black pepper

COOK'S TIP
*Use sun-dried tomato paste for
extra flavor, if you like.*

Heat 2 tablespoons of the tomato oil, add the onion, garlic and chilies and fry gently for about 5 minutes until soft. Add the sun-dried tomatoes, chopped tomatoes and tomato paste to the pan and season to taste. Bring to a boil, then simmer uncovered, stirring occasionally, for 15 minutes.

Remove the stalks from the spinach, rinse the leaves and pat dry with paper towels. Chop the spinach and stir it into the sauce. Cook, stirring, for 5–10 minutes, until the spinach has wilted and no excess moisture remains. Let cool. Preheat the oven to 425°F.

Brush the pizza crust with the remaining oil, then spoon on the sauce. Scatter with the cheeses and bake for 15–20 minutes, until crisp and golden.

CHILI CON CARNE

An all-time favorite, this hot and spicy dish uses both fresh chilies and chili powder.

Serves 8

3 tablespoons vegetable oil

1 large onion, chopped

2 fresh red chilies, seeded and sliced

2 pounds ground beef

4 garlic cloves, crushed

1 tablespoon light brown sugar

2–3 tablespoons chili powder

1 teaspoon ground cumin

1 teaspoon each salt and ground
*   black pepper*

5-ounce can tomato paste

1 cup beer

4 tomatoes, cooked and sieved

2 cups cooked or canned red
*   kidney beans, rinsed*
*   and drained*

salt

To serve

1 pound spaghetti, broken in half

1 cup sour cream

2 cups grated Cheddar or Gruyère
*   cheese*

Heat the oil in a deep saucepan and cook the onion and chilies for about 5 minutes, until softened. Add the beef and cook until browned, breaking up the meat with the side of a spoon.

Stir in the garlic, brown sugar, chili powder, cumin, salt and pepper. Add the tomato paste, beer and sieved tomatoes. Stir to mix. Bring to a boil, then reduce the heat, cover and simmer for 50 minutes.

Stir in the kidney beans and simmer for 5 more minutes, uncovered.

Meanwhile, cook the spaghetti in a large saucepan of boiling salted water until just tender (check package instructions for cooking time). Drain.

To serve, put the spaghetti into a warmed bowl. Ladle the chili over the spaghetti and top with some of the sour cream and grated cheese. Serve the remaining sour cream and cheese separately, if desired.

Piquant Vegetable Dishes

Stir-fries, stuffed bell peppers and spicy vegetable mixes just beg the bite that only chilies can give. If your repertoire of vegetarian recipes seems a little dull, here's the solution!

BEAN CURD AND CHILI STIR-FRY

Fresh green chilies add a fiery heat to the bean curd and crunchy vegetables in this stir-fry.

Serves 2–4

4 ounces hard white cabbage

2 fresh green chilies

8 ounces firm bean curd

3 tablespoons vegetable oil

2 garlic cloves, crushed

3 scallions, chopped

6 ounces green beans, trimmed

6 ounces baby corn, halved

4 ounces beansprouts

3 tablespoons smooth peanut butter

1½ tablespoons dark soy sauce

1¼ cups coconut milk, to serve

COOK'S TIP

Make sure you buy firm bean curd which is easy to cut neatly. Try smoked bean curd for a change.

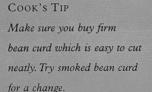

Shred the white cabbage. Carefully remove the seeds and chop the chilies finely. Cut the bean curd into strips.

Heat the wok, then add 2 tablespoons of the oil. When the oil is hot, add the bean curd, stir-fry for 3 minutes and remove with a slotted spoon. Set aside. Wipe out the wok with paper towels.

Add the remaining oil to the wok. When it is hot, add the garlic, scallions and chilies and stir-fry for 1 minute. Add the cabbage, green beans, corn and beansprouts and stir-fry for 2 more minutes.

Add the peanut butter and soy sauce and stir to coat. Return the bean curd to the wok, heat through for 1 minute and serve with the coconut milk.

SPICED VEGETABLES WITH COCONUT

This substantial dish, spiced with fresh red chili, is ideal as a vegetarian main course or as an appetizer for four.

Serves 2

2 large carrots

6 stalks celery

1 fennel bulb

2 tablespoons grapeseed oil

1-inch piece fresh ginger,
  peeled and grated

1 garlic clove, crushed

1 fresh red chili, seeds removed

3 scallions, sliced

14-ounce can coconut milk

1 tablespoon chopped fresh cilantro

salt and ground black pepper

cilantro sprigs, to garnish

S lice the carrots and the celery sticks on the diagonal. Trim the fennel and slice roughly, using a sharp knife. Heat the wok, then add the oil. When the oil is hot, add the ginger, garlic, chili, carrots, celery, fennel and scallions. Stir-fry for 2 minutes.

Stir in the coconut milk with a large spoon and bring to a boil. Lower the heat and simmer for 2 minutes. Add the chopped cilantro and seasoning to taste. Serve immediately, garnished with fresh cilantro.

COOK'S TIP
Reserve any green fronds from the fennel bulb to use as a feathery garnish.

48

POTATOES WITH RED CHILIES

New potatoes absorb the chili flavor wonderfully in this fiery-hot, easy-to-make vegetarian dish.

Serves 4

12–14 new potatoes, scrubbed
  and halved

2 tablespoons vegetable oil

½ teaspoon crushed dried
  red chilies

½ teaspoon white cumin seeds

½ teaspoon fennel seeds

½ teaspoon crushed coriander seeds

1 tablespoon salt

1 onion, sliced

1–4 fresh red chilies, chopped

1 tablespoon chopped fresh cilantro

COOK'S TIP

Four red chilies may be too fiery for some palates. For a milder version, either seed the chilies or use fewer. Experiment with the strength to find the perfect flavor balance for your family.

Bring a saucepan of water to a boil. Add the potatoes and boil for about 15 minutes, until tender but still firm. Drain well, return the potatoes to the dry pan and cover with two sheets of paper towels to absorb any remaining moisture.

Heat the oil in a deep frying pan, then fry the crushed chilies, all the seeds and the salt for 30–40 seconds over medium heat.

Add the sliced onion and fry until golden brown. Then add the potatoes, fresh red chilies and fresh cilantro. Cover and cook for 5–7 minutes over very low heat. Serve immediately.

CHILI-STUFFED PEPPERS

This famous Indian dish is made with fresh green chilies. Hot, spicy and extremely delicious, it is best prepared several days in advance with extra oil to allow the spices to mature.

Serves 4–6

1 tablespoon sesame seeds

1 tablespoon white poppy seeds,
* if available*

1 teaspoon coriander seeds

¼ cup dry shredded coconut

½ onion, sliced

1-inch piece fresh ginger, sliced

4 garlic cloves, sliced

a handful cilantro leaves

6 fresh green chilies

¼ cup vegetable oil

2 potatoes, boiled and roughly mashed

salt, to taste

2 each green, red and yellow bell
* peppers*

2 tablespoons sesame oil

1 teaspoon cumin seeds

¼ cup tamarind juice

fresh green chilies, to garnish

In a frying pan, dry-fry the seeds, then add the coconut and continue to roast until it is golden brown. Add the onion, ginger, garlic, cilantro and 2 of the chilies and roast for 5 more minutes. Cool, then grind to a paste using a mortar and pestle, food processor or blender. Set aside.

Heat 2 tablespoons of the vegetable oil in the frying pan and fry the ground paste for 4–5 minutes. Add the potatoes and salt and stir well.

Slice the stalk ends off the peppers and reserve for lids. Remove the seeds and any white pith. Fill with the potato mixture and replace the lids.

Heat the sesame oil and remaining vegetable oil in the clean frying pan and fry the cumin seeds and the remaining chilies. When the chilies change color, add the tamarind juice and bring to a boil. Stand the peppers in the mixture, cover the pan and cook until the peppers are tender. Serve hot or at room temperature, garnished with fresh chilies.

GREEN LIMA BEANS IN CHILI SAUCE

Colorful and fizzing with flavor, this Mexican vegetable dish uses hot jalapeño chilies.

Serves 4

*1 pound green lima or fava beans,
  thawed if frozen*

2 tablespoons olive oil

1 onion, finely chopped

2 garlic cloves, chopped

*3 large tomatoes, peeled, seeded
  and chopped*

*1–2 drained canned jalapeño chilies,
  seeded and chopped*

salt, to taste

fresh cilantro sprigs, to garnish

COOK'S TIP
*Any green beans are delicious
cooked like this. Try Kenyan
fine beans or Egyptian bobby
beans for a change.*

Bring a saucepan of lightly salted water to a boil. Add the beans and cook for 15–20 minutes, until tender. Drain and return to the dry pan. Cover tightly to keep the beans hot.

Heat the olive oil in a frying pan and sauté the onion and garlic until the onion is soft but not brown. Add the tomatoes and cook until the mixture is thick and flavorful. Add the jalapeños and cook for 1–2 minutes. Season with salt.

Pour the mixture over the reserved beans, mix lightly and spoon into a warmed serving dish. Garnish with the cilantro and serve.

CHILAQUILES

Fried tortilla strips layered with a tomatillo sauce spiced with jalapeños make an unusual vegetarian dish.

Serves 4

¼ cup corn or peanut oil

6 freshly prepared unbaked corn
   tortillas, cut or torn into
   ½-inch strips

10-ounce can tomatillos (Mexican
   green tomatoes)

1 onion, finely chopped

2–3 drained canned jalapeño chilies,
   rinsed, seeded and chopped

2 tablespoons chopped fresh cilantro

1 cup grated Cheddar cheese

¾ cup vegetable stock

salt and ground black pepper

To garnish

sliced onion, stuffed green olives
   and chopped fresh cilantro

Heat 3 tablespoons of the oil in a large frying pan. Fry the tortilla strips, a few at a time, on both sides without browning. Add more oil if needed. Drain on paper towels.

Put the tomatillos and their juice into a food processor or blender. Add the onion, chilies and cilantro. Season with salt and pepper to taste. Process to a smooth purée.

Preheat the oven to 350°F. Heat the remaining oil in a clean frying pan, add the tomatillo mixture and cook gently for 2–3 minutes, stirring frequently.

Pour a layer of the sauce into the bottom of a shallow baking dish, cover with a layer of tortilla strips, then sprinkle on a layer of grated cheese. Continue layering until all the ingredients have been used, reserving some of the cheese for sprinkling on top.

Pour the vegetable stock over the dish and sprinkle with the reserved cheese. Bake for 30 minutes, or until heated through.

Serve directly from the dish, garnished with sliced onion, stuffed green olives and cilantro.

Spicy Salsas, Sauces and Relishes

The role of chilies is to add accent, and these wonderful dips, pickles and salsas do precisely that. For glorious color and flavor, Chili and Red Pepper Jelly is the perfect choice.

TOMATO AND CHILI SALSA

Canned green chilies add zip to this salsa, which is good for livening up grilled meats, fish and shellfish.

Makes 4 cups

1 fresh hot green chili, chopped

1 garlic clove

½ red onion, roughly chopped

3 scallions, chopped

¼ cup fresh cilantro leaves, plus
* extra, to garnish*

1½ pound ripe tomatoes, seeded and
* roughly chopped*

1–3 drained canned green chilies

1 tablespoon olive oil

2 tablespoons fresh lime or lemon juice

½ teaspoon salt, or to taste

2-3 tablespoons tomato juice

Combine the fresh green chili, garlic, red onion, scallions and cilantro in a food processor or blender. Process until finely chopped.

Add the tomatoes, canned chilies, olive oil, lime or lemon juice, salt and tomato juice. Pulse until just chopped; the salsa should be chunky.

Transfer to a bowl and taste for seasoning. Cover and let sit for at least 30 minutes before serving. This salsa is best served the day it is made. Garnish with cilantro.

COOK'S TIP
For less heat, remove the seeds from both the fresh and the canned chilies.

BELL PEPPER AND CHILI SAUCE

This warming sauce, made with both chili powder and fresh chili, is ideal to spice up pasta.

Serves 3–4

2 tablespoons olive oil

1 onion, chopped

1 fresh red chili, seeded and sliced
  (optional)

1 garlic clove, crushed

2 large red or orange bell peppers,
  seeded and finely chopped

1 teaspoon chili powder or sweet
  chili sauce

1 tablespoon paprika

½ teaspoon dried thyme

8-ounce can chopped tomatoes

1¼ cups vegetable stock

½ teaspoon sugar

salt and ground black pepper

2 tablespoons drained sun-dried
  tomatoes in oil, chopped

lettuce, to garnish

freshly cooked pasta, to serve

Heat the oil in a saucepan. Add the onion, fresh chili (if using), garlic and red or orange bell peppers. Sauté for 4–5 minutes or until the mixture is lightly browned.

Add the chili powder or sweet chili sauce with the paprika and thyme, and cook for 1 more minute.

Stir in the tomatoes, vegetable stock and sugar, with salt and pepper to taste. Bring to a boil. Cover, lower the heat and simmer for 20 minutes, adding more stock if necessary.

Stir in the sun-dried tomatoes and cook for 10 minutes or until the tomatoes are tender and the sauce is thick and flavorful. Serve immediately, with freshly cooked pasta, garnished with lettuce.

CHILI AND COCONUT SALSA

This sweet-and-sour salsa, with the fiery heat of green chilies, goes well with grilled or barbecued fish.

Serves 6–8

1 small coconut

1 small pineapple

2 fresh green chilies

2-inch piece lemongrass

¼ cup plain yogurt

½ teaspoon salt

2 tablespoons chopped cilantro

cilantro sprigs, to garnish

Puncture two of the coconut eyes with a screwdriver and drain the milk from the shell and discard. Crack the coconut shell, remove the flesh, then coarsely grate the coconut into a bowl.

Cut the rind from the pineapple with a sharp knife and remove the eyes with a potato peeler. Finely chop the flesh and add to the coconut together with any juice from the pineapple.

Cut the chilies in half lengthwise and remove the stalks, seeds and membrane. Chop very finely and stir into the coconut mixture.

Finely chop the lemongrass. Stir into the coconut mixture, then add the yogurt, salt and cilantro. Mix well. Spoon into a serving dish and garnish with the cilantro sprigs. Serve the salsa with grilled or barbecued fish, if desired.

COOK'S TIP

The easiest way to chop the lemongrass is to use a large, sharp cook's knife, placing it at right angles to the cutting surface. Keeping the tip steady, move the handle up and down to shave off fine pieces of lemongrass.

GREEN CHILI PICKLE

This wonderful pickle comes with a warning: many small green chilies make it extremely hot.

Makes about 1½ pounds

½ cup yellow mustard seeds, crushed

½ cup ground cumin

¼ cup ground turmeric

4 large garlic cloves, crushed, plus
    20 small garlic cloves, peeled and
    left whole

⅔ cup white vinegar

¾ cup sugar

2 teaspoons salt

⅔ cup mustard oil

1 pound small fresh green chilies,
    halved

COOK'S TIP

Keep a window open while cooking with mustard oil as it is pungent and the smoke may irritate the eyes.

Mix the mustard seeds, ground cumin, turmeric, crushed garlic, white vinegar, sugar and salt in a sterilized glass bowl. Cover with a cloth and let rest for 24 hours. This enables the spices to infuse and the sugar and salt to dissolve.

Heat the mustard oil in a frying pan and gently fry the spice mixture for about 5 minutes (see Cook's Tip). Add the whole garlic cloves and fry for 5 more minutes.

Stir in the chilies and cook gently until tender but still green in color. This will take about 30 minutes over low heat. Cool thoroughly and pour into sterilized bottles, ensuring that the oil is evenly distributed if you are using more than one bottle. Let steep for a week before serving.

CHILI AND GINGER DIP

Red chilies and ginger make up this hot and spicy dip. It is good with vegetables, chicken or seafood.

Makes about 1 cup

½ cup sunflower oil

¼ cup toasted sesame oil

1-inch piece fresh
  ginger, peeled

1–2 garlic cloves, crushed

2 scallions, finely chopped

2 red chilies, seeded and
  finely chopped

crudités, to serve

COOK'S TIP

Medium-size shrimp are ideal served with this sauce. Remove the shell but leave the tails intact so that there is something to hold on to when dipping.

In a small saucepan, gently heat the sunflower oil with the sesame oil. Cut the ginger into thin slices. Stack the slices and cut them into long thin julienne strips. Turn the strips and cut horizontally into very small dice. Put the diced ginger, garlic, scallions and chilies into the oil. Heat for 5–7 minutes to allow the flavors to infuse. Cool and pour the mixture into a small bowl. Serve with crudités.

CHILI AND RED PEPPER JELLY

This sweet-savory jelly, made with red hot chilies, is good with pork, lamb and duck. It would also make an unusual addition to a casual, cold lunch, alongside a sharp Cheddar cheese.

Makes about 3 pounds

2¼ pounds apples

juice of 1 lemon

4½ cups sugar

*4 ounces fresh red chilies, seeded and
    roughly chopped*

*1 large red bell pepper, seeded and
    roughly chopped*

1 large Spanish onion, chopped

1½ cups cider vinegar

COOK'S TIP

*Store the jelly in a cool place
and it should keep for up to
one year.*

Cut each apple into about eight pieces, discarding only the bruised and damaged sections, not the cores, peel, seeds or stems. Put into a deep saucepan with the lemon juice and 4 cups cold water. Bring to a boil, lower the heat, cover and simmer for 30 minutes.

Line a colander with a clean dish towel and set it over a deep bowl. Pour the apples and liquid into it and let drip through undisturbed.

Discard the apple debris and pour the liquid into a preserving pan with 3½ cups of the sugar. Stir over low heat until the sugar dissolves completely and the liquid clears. Raise the heat and boil without stirring until a little of the syrup, spread on a cold plate, wrinkles when you push it with your finger. Start testing after 15 minutes, but anticipate that it may take 30 minutes.

Meanwhile, either mince or process the red chilies, red bell pepper and onion together to create a fine hash. Scrape the mixture into a large saucepan and stir in the vinegar and remaining sugar. Heat gently until the sugar dissolves, then raise the heat and boil for 5 minutes. Add to the apple syrup and once again boil until the mixture passes the wrinkle test.

Ladle the hot jelly into hot sterilized jars, cover with vinegar-proof disks and lids and cool for about 20 minutes, then turn the jars upside down to redistribute the flecks of pepper. After 20 more minutes turn them the right way up to finish cooling. Wipe away any external stickiness with a hot damp cloth, then label the jars.

INDEX